Carl Nielsen

THE FOG IS LIFTING

Opus 41

EDITION WILHELM HANSEN AS

Der Nebel Steigt

Aus Helge Rode's Schauspiel
"DIE MUTTER"
für Flöte und Klavier oder Harpe

The Fog is Lifting

From Helge Rode's play
"THE MOTHER"
for Flute and Piano or Harp

Carl Nielsen, Op. 41

27023

Der Nebel Steigt

Aus Helge Rode's Schauspiel
"DIE MUTTER"
für Flöte und Klavier oder Harpe

The Fog is Lifting

From Helge Rode's play
"THE MOTHER"
for Flute and Piano or Harp

Carl Nielsen, Op. 41